A Cozy Christmas Tea

PAINTINGS BY

Sandy Lynam Clough

HARVEST HOUSE PUBLISHERS
EUGENE, OREGON 97402

A Cozy Christmas Tea

The spirit of Christmas

enfolds hearts and homes in warmth as friends come together to
celebrate a time of giving. Gathering for a delightful cup of tea, we
share our memories, laughter, and friendship, knowing that the best
gifts are those that come from the heart. Come celebrate the joy and
peace of this season...with a cozy Christmas tea!

MENU FOR

A Cozy Christmas Tea

ORANGE-
CRANBERRY TEA

4 cups cranberry juice
3 herbal orange tea bags
thinly sliced orange wedges

Heat cranberry juice to almost boiling. Place tea bags
into the pot to steep for 3 to 5 minutes.
Serve in mugs with orange wedges for garnish.

ALMOND COOKIE WREATHS

1 cup sugar
1 cup butter
½ cup milk
1 egg
1 teaspoon vanilla
1 teaspoon almond extract

3½ cups flour
1 teaspoon baking powder
¼ teaspoon salt
½ teaspoon green food coloring
red candied cherries

Mix sugar, butter, milk, egg, vanilla, and almond extract. Stir in flour, baking powder, and salt. Divide dough into halves. Tint one half with green food color. Cover and refrigerate at least four hours.

To make wreaths, roll teaspoonfuls of each colored dough into 4-inch rolls by rolling back and forth on a sugared surface. Place 1 green and 1 white rope side by side, press together lightly and twist for a spiral effect. Form a circle by putting the ends together. Press bits of candied cherries on each wreath for holly berries. Place on ungreased cookie sheet. Heat oven to 350 degrees. Bake for 9 to 12 minutes until set and very light brown. Yields about 4½ dozen cookies.

Surely Everyone

is aware of the divine pleasure which

attend a wintry fireside: candles at

four o'clock, warm hearthrugs, tea,

a fair tea-maker, shutters closed,

curtains flowing in ample draperies

to the floor, whilst the wind and

the rain are raging audibly without.

THOMAS DEQUINCEY

Our hearts they hold all Christmas dear,
And earth seems sweet and heaven seems near.

MARJORIE L.C. PICKETHALL

Christmas isn't a season.
It's a feeling.

EDNA
FERKER

A present

Sandy Lynam Clough

Christmas Eve

was a night of song that wrapped

itself about you like a shawl.

But it warmed more than

your body. It warmed your

heart . . . filled it, too, with melody

that would last forever.

BESS STREETER ALDRICH

Angels

come down,
with Christmas in
their hearts,

Gentle, whimsical,
    laughing, heaven-sent;

And, for a day, fair
    peace have given me.

VACHEL LINDSAY

Glory to God
in the highest,
and on earth
peace to men on
whom his favor rests.

THE BOOK OF LUKE

Sandy Lynam Clough

SCONES

The secret of tender scones is a minimum of handling.

2 cups flour
1 tablespoon baking powder
¼ teaspoon salt
4 tablespoons sugar
6 tablespoons butter
2 eggs, beaten
⅓ cup cream, milk, or half-and-half

In a mixing bowl, combine dry ingredients. With a pastry blender or two knives, cut in butter until mixture resembles coarse crumbs. In a separate bowl, combine eggs and cream until well-blended. Stir cream mixture into dry ingredients until they are moistened. Do not mix the dough for too long or the scones will be hard.

Divide the dough into two 8-inch rounds on a greased baking sheet. Cut the dough with a sharp knife into 8 wedges. Brush the top with milk and sprinkle on sugar. Bake at 400 degrees for 10 to 15 minutes or until the scones are golden brown.

TASTY ADDITIONS FOR SCONES:
2 teaspoons lemon or orange rind
½ cup semi-sweet chocolate chips
½ cup finely chopped nuts
¼ cup cranberries or currants

MOCK DEVONSHIRE CREAM

This is a lovely substitute for English clotted cream.
In a pinch, commercial whipped topping may be used.

½ cup heavy cream
or 8 ounces softened cream cheese

2 tablespoons confectioners' sugar

½ cup sour cream

Using a chilled bowl, beat cream until medium-stiff peaks form. Add the sugar in the last few minutes of beating. (If using cream cheese, just mix in sugar.) Fold in sour cream and blend. Makes 1½ cups.

Beth played her gayest march, Amy threw open the door, and
Meg enacted escort with great dignity. Mrs. March was both
surprised and touched, and smiled with her eyes full as she
examined her presents and read the little notes which
accompanied them....There was a good deal of laughing and
kissing and explaining, in the simple, loving fashion which
makes these home festivals so pleasant at the time, so sweet
to remember long afterward....

LOUISA MAY ALCOTT

Little Women

Giving presents is a talent: to know what a person wants,
to know when and how to get it, to give it lovingly and well.

PAMELA GLENCONNER

Somehow not only for

Christmas

but all the long year through,

The joy that you give

others is the joy that

comes back to you.

JOHN GREENLEAF
WHITTIER

18

*It is possible to give without loving,
but it is impossible to love without giving.*

RICHARD BRAUNSTEIN

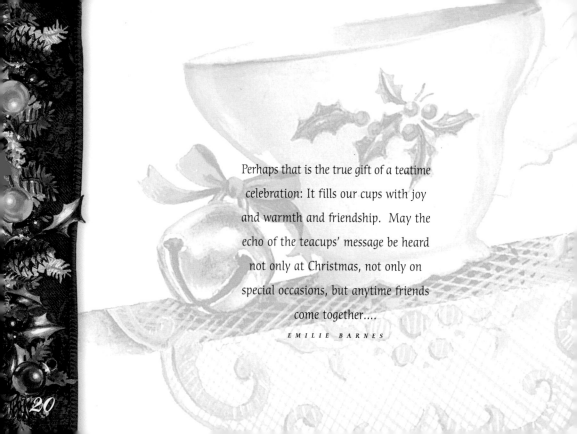

Perhaps that is the true gift of a teatime
celebration: It fills our cups with joy
and warmth and friendship. May the
echo of the teacups' message be heard
not only at Christmas, not only on
special occasions, but anytime friends
come together....

EMILIE BARNES

20

Tea pot is on, the cups are waiting,
Favorite chairs anticipating,
No matter what I have to do,
My friend there's always time for you.

ANONYMOUS

EGG SALAD
SANDWICHES

4 hard-boiled eggs, finely chopped
¼ cup mayonnaise
3 tablespoons sweet pickles, finely chopped
1 tablespoon mustard
salt and pepper to taste

Combine all ingredients in a mixing bowl until well blended.
Chill until ready to make sandwiches. Spread on bread.
Sandwiches can be cut into tree shapes for a more festive look.

EGGNOG HOLIDAY BREAD

3 cups flour, sifted
¾ cup sugar
1 tablespoon baking powder
1 teaspoon salt
½ teaspoon nutmeg
1½ cups dairy eggnog
1 egg, beaten
¼ cup butter, melted
¾ cup pecans, chopped
¾ cup candied fruit

In a large bowl, sift together flour, sugar, baking powder, salt, and nutmeg. In a separate bowl, mix eggnog, egg, and butter. Add wet ingredients to dry, stirring well. Add pecans and fruit. Bake in greased loaf pan at 350 degrees for 60 to 70 minutes. Cool on a wire rack.

Heap on more wood!
—the wind is chill;
But let it whistle
as it will,
We'll keep our

Christmas

merry still.

SIR WALTER SCOTT

Sandy Lynam Clough

Anne peeped out from her frosted gable window with delighted eyes. The firs in the Haunted Wood were all feathery and wonderful; the birches and wild cherry-trees were outlined in pearl; the ploughed fields were stretches of snowy dimples; and there was a crisp tang in the air that was glorious...."Merry Christmas, Marilla! Merry Christmas, Matthew! Isn't it a lovely Christmas?"

L . M .   M O N T G O M E R Y
A n n e   o f   G r e e n   G a b l e s

Outdoors, the sun was shining on the snow. The icicles twinkled all along the eaves. Far away sleigh-bells faintly jingled....

L A U R A   I N G A L L S   W I L D E R
F a r m e r   B o y

And there were shepherds living out in the fields
nearby, keeping watch over their flocks at night.
An angel of the Lord appeared to them, and the
glory of the Lord shown around them....

THE BOOK OF LUKE

Father, may that Holy star
Grow every year more bright,
And send its glorious beams afar
To fill the world with light.

WILLIAM CULLEN BRYANT

28

"...I am sure I have always

thought of

Christmas time...

as a good time:

a kind, forgiving, charitable,

pleasant time....I believe that

it has done me good,

and will do me good; and I say,

God bless it!"

CHARLES DICKENS
A Christmas Carol

*Blessed by the
Christmas sunshine, our natures,
perhaps: long leafless, bring forth
new love, new kindness, new
mercy, new compassion.*

HELEN KELLER

May you have the
gladness of Christmas
Which is hope;
The spirit of Christmas
Which is peace;
The heart of Christmas
Which is love.

ADA V. HENDRICKS